THE SUSHI HANDBOOK

A Guide to Eating Japan's Favorite Delicacy

by Kenji Kumagai

HEIAN

Second printing 1985

Heian International, Inc.
P.O. Box 1013
Union City, CA 94587
U.S.A.

We acknowledge the help of Yuzo Hirata
(Sushi-Yu, Kyoto, Japan) in the preparation
of the photographs used in this book.

ISBN: 0-89346-211-X

Printed in Japan

Welcome to the world of *sushi*!

The sushi-maker scoops up just the right amount of rice, deftly molds it into shape, spreads some horseradish on a slice of fish, places the rice on the fish, turns it over . . . and it is finished!

You enjoy the beauty and color of the finished product for a few moments, then dip it in some soy sauce and pop it into your mouth. Delicious!

This is the entire world of sushi. And yet in this most elementary exchange is contained the essense of Japanese art and culture.

The primary characteristic of traditional Japanese culture is simplicity and transiency. How much simpler can you get than satisfying a basic human need, eating, and how much more transient than eating the art object after looking at it for just a few moments?

Sushi was introduced into Japan from the greater Asian continent but, like everything imported into Japan, was made uniquely Japanese. It took hundreds of years for sushi to evolve into its present form, and during that time, a complete etiquette for eating it developed.

This little volume introduces you to the fascinating world of eating sushi. It will not make you a *tsu* (sushi expert), but it will give you a start.

Welcome, or as we say in Japanese, *irrasshai-masse*!

CONTENTS

ILLUSTRATIONS

ORIGINS

BEGINNINGS

There are several theories about the origin of *sushi*. The most likely is that it developed in the mountainous areas of Southeast Asia. The people in that area soaked the occasional fish they caught, in rice. The lactic acid created from the fermentation of fish in rice prevented the fish from going bad. Sushi thus originated as a method of preserving fish.

This technique of preserving fish was probably brought to Japan about the beginning of the first millenium, together with knowledge of rice planting.

A more colorful Japanese tradition of how this method of preserving fish was discovered concerns an old fisherman's wife. It is said she saw an osprey building a nest and placed some leftover rice in the nest. When the old woman looked in the nest some time later, she found the osprey had placed much fish in it. She took the fish home and found it both tasty and that it kept for some time.

The oldest record we have of sushi is contained in a work written during the Nara period (710-795 A.D.). Sushi was then considered to be just a method of preserving fish. Sea food was sprinkled with salt and pressed. The fermentation after several months acted as a preservative, similar to salting fish today.

At any rate, the acidy taste produced by the fermentation was called sushi, and that is how sushi is said to have been named. The character used to write sushi meaning acidy is different from the character or characters used to write sushi, the subject of this handbook. The word sushi can be written in many ways. Figure 1 illustrates some of the characters that can be used.

Later, rice was used in place of salt to "cure" or "ripen" fish. The Japanese word for "ripen" is *narasu*, and so this form of foodstuff began to be called *nare-zushi*. In nare-zushi, rice is used only to "ripen" the fish and is discarded when the fish is eaten.

Nare-zushi is still made in rural areas of Japan using local seafood.

Sometimes the fish and rice combination was put under pressure to hasten the "ripening" process. Stones were used to create the pressure, so this was referred to as *ishi-zushi*, "rock" sushi.

FIGURE 1. WAYS OF WRITING THE WORD "SUSHI"

すし

This is sushi written using the *hiragana* syllabary attributed to the great Shingon Buddhist master, Kobo *Daishi*. These letters have no meanings associated with them, and can only be read su-shi.

寿し 壽し

The first *kanji* Chinese character by itself is read *kotobuki* and means "long life." When used in combination, it can be read *su*. The second letter is the *hiragana* letter *shi*. The first *kanji* to the left is the "reformed" *toyo kanji* form adopted by the Japanese government under the MacArthur occupation, and the *kanji* to the right is the same character written in the traditional way.

壽司

The second *kanji* of this way of writing sushi means "official." Both these *kanji* are used only for their sounds and not the meanings associated with them.

酢鮨

These two *kanji* originally meant jellyfish (*kanji* to the left) and a type of shark, but in modern Japanese both are read and mean only sushi.

酸し

This is the way to write the word sushi meaning "acidy."

NAMA-NARE-ZUSHI

About the latter part of the Muromachi period (1333-1573 A.D.), it became apparent that fish could be eaten fresh with the rice made "acidy" with vinegar. This is the forerunner of what is today known as *nama-nare-zushi*.

Nare-zushi, which was eaten from the Nara period, was considered to be an appetizer but nama-nare-zushi became the main course because rice is a large part of this dish.

Nama-nare-zushi is still made in rural areas of Wakayama Prefecture, primarily with mackerel.

MODERN-DAY SUSHI

Tokugawa Iyeyasu founded his Bakufu government in Edo (the ancient name for present-day Tokyo) in 1603, but the center of culture for the first few years remained in the ancient capital city of Kyoto. There, *nama-nare-zushi,* the form of sushi created during the Muromachi period, remained popular.

Sushi to meet the needs of the new age of the Tokugawa rule was created in Edo during the 1670's.

A physician named Matsumoto Yoshito created something called *haya-zushi* ("fast" sushi). What set haya-zushi apart from other forms of sushi is that it was prepared while the customer waited.

The shops where haya-zushi was sold were called *tachi-gui*, literally, "stand-and-eat," and were the first fast-food establishments in Japan. The speed of service perfectly suited the temperament of the *Edokko* (child of Edo), as the inhabitants of Edo were proud of calling themselves. The addresses of two tachi-guis are listed in a work about Edo published as early as the 1680's.

Haya-zushi reached the height of its popularity during the 1770's.

Other forms of sushi developed from haya-zushi. These include:

- *Hana-zushi* - Sushi made with soy-bean curd residue.
- *Hako-zushi* - "Box" Sushi.
- *Okashi-zushi* - "Confectionary" Sushi.
- *Chirashi-zushi* - "Scattered" Sushi.
- *Mushi-zushi* - "Steamed" Sushi.
- *Maki-zushi* - "Rolled" Sushi.

3

- *Temaki-zushi* - "Hand-rolled" Sushi.
- *Inari-zushi* - Fried bean-curd stuffed with vinegared rice.

These forms of sushi are described in a little more detail in Table 1.

TABLE 1. **TYPES OF SUSHI**

Type	Description
Chirashi-zushi ("Scattered" Sushi)	Vinegared rice placed in a box, on top of which is placed fish or other ingredients. This sushi is eaten from the box, using chopsticks. A bowl is often used instead of a box.
Hako-zushi or *Oshi-zushi* ("Box" or "Pressed" Sushi)	Developed in the Osaka area. Consists of vinegared rice placed in a box, on top of which fish or other ingredients are placed. The rice/fish in the box is pressed, removed, and cut into bite-size pieces, like a cake.
Inari-zushi	Deep-fried bean curd *(abura-age)* stuffed with vinegared rice in which vegetables are often mixed.
Maki-zushi ("Rolled" Sushi)	Vinegared rice rolled in a sheet of dried seaweed *(nori)*, with ingredients in the middle and sliced. In the Osaka area, *maki-zushi* is characterized by its thinness. In the Tokyo area, it is called *futo-maki* ("thick" roll), and contains more rice and more ingredients in the center than the Osaka style.
Mushi-zushi ("Steamed" Sushi)	Vinegared rice with fish or other ingredients on top, placed in a box with a net-like bottom. The box is placed over a container of boiling water to steam the contents.

TABLE 1. **TYPES OF SUSHI** (Continued)

Type	Description
Nama-nare-zushi ("Raw-ripened" Sushi)	Holdover from the oldest form of sushi, and today is found mostly in rural areas of Japan. Few sushi bars serve this.
Nigiri- or *Edomae-zushi* ("Grasped" or "In front of Edo" Sushi)	The most popular form of sushi. Developed in the Edo (Tokyo) area. Consists of a hand-molded piece of vinegared rice placed on fish or other ingredient.
Okashi-zushi ("Confectionary" Sushi)	Vinegared rice placed in a small mold, on top of which fish or other ingredients are placed, and pressed. The pressed ingredients are removed and placed with other such pieces to form a design.
Temaki-zushi ("Hand-rolled" Sushi)	Vinegared rice rolled in a sheet of dried seaweed *(nori),* with ingredients in the middle. Differs from *maki-zushi* in that the roll is made by hand without the use of a *makisu* (see "Making Maki-zushi"), and not sliced.
Hana-zushi (Sushi made with soy-bean residue)	Vinegared rice on which the residue from making soy-bean curds *(tofu)* is placed.

NIGIRI-ZUSHI

A food even more basic to the Japanese diet than sushi is *nigiri-meshi,* literally, "grasp" or "to grab," and "rice." Nigiri-meshi is a handful of plain boiled rice in which a bit of *umeboshi* (pickled plum) or other flavored edible is placed.

In Japan, nigiri-meshi is the equivalent of the sandwich in the West. In particular, nigiri-meshi with an umeboshi in the center is very popular. This form of nigiri-meshi is called *hi-no-maru-bento,* literally, "sun-circle-lunch." The red umeboshi inside the white rice may very well have inspired the design of the modern Japanese flag.

It was inevitable that the sushi and nigiri-meshi traditions would meet. A man named Hanaya Yohei is credited with creating nigiri-zushi during the 1820's. Putting slices of seafood on vinegared balls of rice could be done very quickly and perfectly suited the Edokko. Nigiri-zushi soon became the rage of Edo and its popularity has continued to this day.

Figure 2 is a chart that shows how sushi developed.

FIGURE 2. DEVELOPMENT OF SUSHI

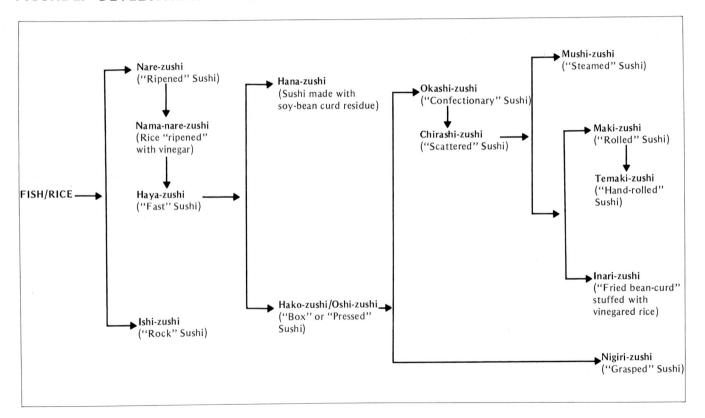

SUSHI

TYPES OF SUSHI

Sushi can broadly be divided into two types. These types are associated with two metropolitan areas in Japan: Edo, the ancient name for present-day Tokyo, and Osaka.

The first type of sushi consists of hand-molded vinegared rice placed on fish or other ingredient, and is called *Edo-mae,* literally, "in front of Edo." The exact derivation of this name is not known, but it seems to have been so named because the fish used to make this type of sushi was caught in Edo (Tokyo) Bay, which is "in front of Edo."

Edomae-zushi is the type made at most sushi bars. An equally popular name for this type of sushi is *nigiri-zushi* ("grasp" sushi) because of how it is made.

The second major type of sushi consists of vinegared rice pressed in a box with fish or other ingredients placed on top. The rice and fish are removed from the box and cut into pieces like a cake. This type of sushi became popular in the Osaka area. Because of the way in which this type of sushi is made, it is called *oshi-zushi* ("pressed" sushi). It is also called *hako-zushi* ("box" sushi) and also *bottera,* which is the Japanese way of pronouncing the Dutch word for "box."

Although *nigiri-zushi* and *oshi-zushi* are associated with the cities of Edo and Osaka, there are other types of sushi that do not take these regional areas into account.

Table 1 lists some of the different types of sushi.

HOW SUSHI IS MADE

Sushi is made from the simplest of materials: rice and fish or other kind of seafood.

If you are the least serious about sushi, you must remember two terms:

- *Shari*
- *Neta,* sometimes called *tane.*

Shari refers to the rice that is molded and placed on the fish or other material to make sushi. *Shari* is not plain rice, but rice delicately flavored with vinegar, *sake,* salt, and sugar.

Neta is the material on which the *shari* is placed. It is the main ingredient of sushi and can be raw fish, omelet, octopus, shrimp, or any of the many things presently being used in making sushi, including avocado.

TYPES OF SHARI

There are three types of *shari*:

- *Usu-aji* ("thin taste"), used primarily to make *nigiri-zushi.* This *shari* is made to complement the taste of fish.
- *Ama-kuchi* ("sweet mouth"), used primarily to make *inari-zushi* and *futo-maki* sushi.
- *Kokuchi-aji* ("thick taste"), used primarily to make *chirashi-zushi.*

The rice is cooked in one batch and flavored with vinegar and a little *sake.* The difference in *shari* is the amount of sugar and salt added, *usu-aji* having the least, *ama-kuchi* a little more, and *kokuchi-aji* the most.

The best *shari* is that which is not noticed. If you are conscious of how tasty the *shari* is, that *shari* is not performing its proper function. This may not be a very good analogy in our day of women's lib, but traditionally *shari* was considered very much like a good wife who is unnoticed but essential to her husband's success.

TYPES OF NETA

Most of the ingredients used to make sushi are used raw. For this reason, what sets a *tsu* (sushi expert) apart from others is his knowledge of neta, the ingredients used to make sushi, rather than knowledge of how neta is prepared.

Figure 3 shows the parts of tuna used as neta. This illustration also applies to any large fish.

Table 2 lists the more commonly-used neta. This is not an exhaustive list. Many neta originate in both Japan and the United States, so the season when the neta is best varies much more than is indicated in this table. When in doubt, ask your sushi-maker what is in season.

FIGURE 3. PARTS OF TUNA USED AS NETA

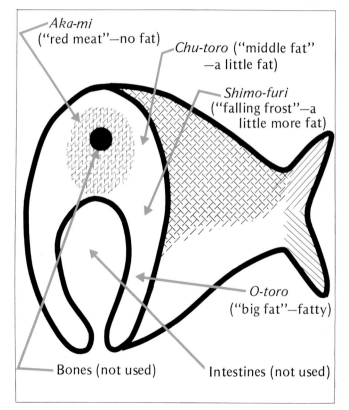

Aka-mi ("red meat"—no fat)

Chu-toro ("middle fat" —a little fat)

Shimo-furi ("falling frost"—a little more fat)

O-toro ("big fat"—fatty)

Bones (not used)

Intestines (not used)

13

TABLE 2. TYPES OF NETA

NETA		ORIGIN	WHEN BEST (APPROX.)
English	Japanese		
Abalone	*Awabi*	USA	July-March
Black Clam	*Tori-gai*	Japan	Dec.-March
Eel	*Unagi*	Japan	May-Sept.
Fatty Tuna	*Toro*	USA	July-Sept.
Fish Roe	*Kazuno-ko*	USA	Dec.-Feb.
Halibut	*Hirame*	USA	Year-round
Herring	*Kohada*	Japan	Aug.-Oct.
Jumbo Clam	*Miru-gai*	USA	Year-round
King Crab	*Kani*	USA	Dec.-March
Mackerel	*Saba*	Japan	Sept.-Nov.
Octopus	*Tako*	USA	Nov.-March
Oyster	*Kaki*	USA	Oct.-March

NETA		ORIGIN	WHEN BEST (APPROX.)
English	Japanese		
Salmon	*Shake*	USA	April-Oct.
Salmon Roe	*Ikura*	USA	Nov.-March
Scallop	*Hotate-gai*	Japan	Dec.-April
Sea Urchin	*Uni*	USA	Year-round
Shrimp	*Ebi*	USA	May-Sept.
Spanish Mackerel	*Aji*	USA	July-Sept.
Squid	*Ika*	USA	Nov.-March
Sweet Shrimp	*Ama-ebi*	USA	Nov.-April
Trough Shell	*Aoyagi*	USA	May-July
Tuna	*Maguro*	USA	July-Sept.
Yellowtail	*Hamachi*	Japan	Year-round

Nigiri-zushi is what is usually thought of when sushi is mentioned, and making it is what is usually thought of as the sushi-maker's art.

The sushi-maker starts by slicing the fish, crab, octopus, or other *neta* that will be used to make the sushi. He then dips his right hand into a solution of water and vinegar, and wets both hands with it. Then he scoops up just the right amount of *shari* with his right hand and half molds it in one quick motion. He then picks up the *neta,* and while holding it in his left hand, spreads horseradish *(wasabi)* on the *neta* with his right index finger (the *shari* is still in his right hand). He places the *shari* on the *neta* and presses down with his right index finger to give the sushi its initial shape, and uses his left thumb to shape the other end. He then rolls the sushi over, shapes both sides with his right thumb and index finger, and then from the top. Finally, he turns the sushi around, gives it a final touch, and it is complete.

Figure 4 illustrates this process.

The *shari* used in *nigiri-zushi* is molded into one of three "classical" forms. These forms may look alike, but to sushi-makers and *tsu* (sushi experts), they are quite distinct. Because every sushi-maker has a different size hand, different length fingers, etc., every sushi-maker has his own interpretation of the classical forms.

The three classical forms are (the forms are as seen from the side):

- *Suehiro-gata,* "folding fan" form:

- *Funa-gata,* "boat" form:

- *Koban-gata,* "koban" form (koban is an old-style Japanese coin):

The forms shown above are somewhat exaggerated to show the differences. In practice, they look much more alike. The most popular forms are *suehiro-gata* and *funa-gata.* The *koban-gata* is usually made in sushi bars where the customers are more interested in quantity than in quality.

FIGURE 4. **MAKING NIGIRI-ZUSHI**

◁1. The sushi-maker dips his right hand into a solution of vinegar and water.

2. He spreads the solution over his hands. ▷

3. He scoops up just the right amount of *shari* with his right hand.

4. While holding the *neta* in his left hand, he dips his right finger into some horseradish *(wasabi)*. ▶

17

6. He places the *shari* on the *neta* and gives the sushi its initial shape by pressing down on the *shari* with his right index finger (not shown), and then using his left and right thumbs to shape the ends. ▶

◀5. He spreads the *wasabi* on the *neta* (the *shari* is still in his right hand).

◀7. He turns the sushi over and shapes both sides with his right thumb and index finger.

8. He turns the sushi around again to give it a final touch. ▶

19

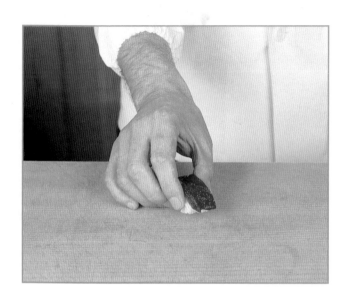

◄9. Finished!

10. Sushi is often served on a platform-like tray called variously, *sushi-dai, mori-dai,* and *tsuke-dai.* ▶

The sushi-maker begins making *maki-zushi* by placing a device made of bamboo strips tied together (a *makisu*) on his counter, and placing a sheet of dried seaweed *(nori)* on it. He then grabs a handful of *shari* and spreads it evenly over the *nori*. Then he spreads horseradish *(wasabi)* on the shari, and places the ingredients *(neta)* on top. Using the *makisu,* he rolls the *nori* from the bottom to form the sushi.

The sushi-maker then wets his knife and slices the roll in half. He places the two half pieces together and slices them in two places, for a total of six pieces. The *maki-zushi* is now ready to be served.

Figure 5 illustrates this process.

FIGURE 5. **MAKING MAKI-ZUSHI**

1. The sushi-maker places a sheet of *nori* (seaweed) on a *makisu*. ▼

2. He grabs a handful of *shari* (about three or four times the amount for a single sushi) and places it on the *nori.*

3. He spreads the *shari* evenly over the *nori.* ▶

◄ 4. He spreads horseradish *(wasabi)* on the *shari*.

5. He places the *neta* in the middle of the *shari*. ▶

6. He begins rolling the *nori* from the bottom.

7. He continues rolling. ▶

24

9. He removes the roll from the *makisu* and wets his knife. ▶

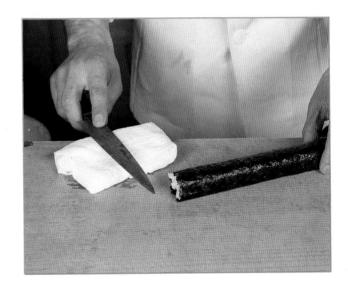

◀8. He firms up the roll.

25

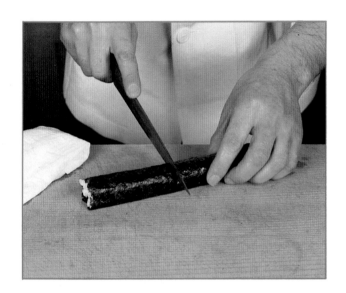

10. He cuts the roll in the middle.

11. He places the two halves together and makes the first of two cuts. ▶

◀12. He makes the second cut.

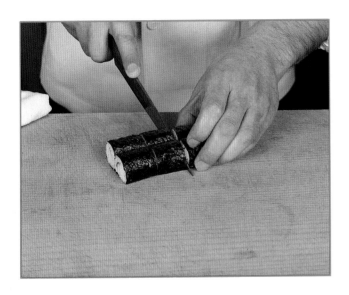

13. He turns the cut pieces over.▶

14. Finished!

15. The completed *maki-zushi* are often placed on a small platform with legs called a *geta*.

THE SUSHI MAKER

The person who makes your sushi is central to its enjoyment. He is called *ita-mae*, which literally means, "in front of counter."

Make a friend of your itamae and rely on his judgement; you will not regret it.

When you refer to an itamae, add the honorific suffix *-san*, thus *itamae-san*. This will demonstrate how polite and civilized you are, and may even result in better service.

The responsibility for setting the standards at a particular sushi bar rests on its head itamae. There is no problem with only one itamae, but with two or more itamae, there must be a lead or head itamae who sets the standard.

The position where the head itamae stands is determined by tradition. He even has a special name. The head itamae stands at the side of the counter furthest from the door. He is called *kami*, which means "up" or "above."

If the door faces the counter, the kami stands to the left as you enter, unless a window is on that side, in which case the kami stands on the side opposite the window.

The next ranking itamae stands next to the kami, and so on, to the lowest-ranking itamae. These persons are called *naka-ita*, which is a contraction of *naka-itamae*, and means "middle itamae."

If a journeyman itamae (a *shimo-ita*) is present, he stands furthest from the kami.

A sushi bar usually has a maximum of four itamae working at a time. More than this number makes it rather crowded.

Because itamae are not as well trained in the United States as in Japan, in American sushi bars the kami often stands in the middle so he can more easily monitor the work of the others. If there are only two itamae, he often stands closest to the door so he can greet his customers.

Figure 6 illustrates the traditional positions taken by the itamae at the counter.

FIGURE 6.   **TRADITIONAL POSITIONS OF ITAMAE AT COUNTER**

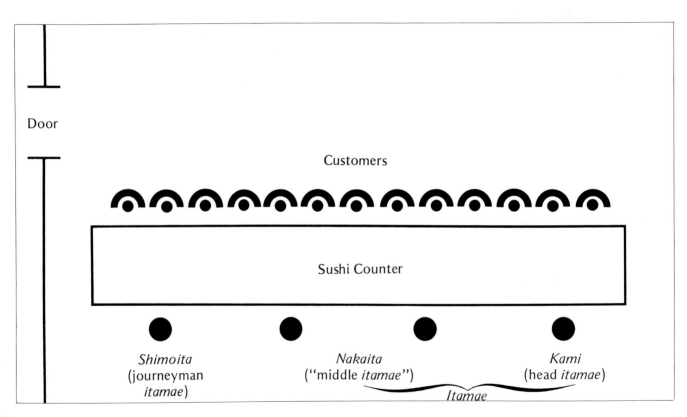

It normally takes seven or eight years to become a full-fledged itamae. The best itamae start right out of high school when they are between 16 and 17 years of age. At this age they are most amenable to being taught the craft of sushi-making. People older than that are rather set in their ways and find it more difficult to accept instructions without bringing their own personalities to their craft.

Master itamae can tell whether another itamae started his apprenticeship at an early age or whether he started later in life.

The itamae apprentice is known as a *minarai*, literally, "learn-by-observing." There are several clearly-defined stages that the minarai goes through.

The first stage, which lasts a year or two, consists of washing the utensils that the itamae use to make sushi, washing dishes, and performing other menial work. Although seemingly unimportant, this part of the apprenticeship is considered very important. You must develop a feel for the tools with which you will work, and there is no better way to get this feel than by washing those tools.

During this first stage, the minarai is called a *decchi-kozo*, a beginning apprentice. The term *kozo* is frequently used in crafts where an apprenticeship is required, and is always the lowest rung in the training program.

After a year or two, the decchi-kozo is promoted to *shikomi*. This usually lasts about three years, during which he prepares the fish for cutting by the itamae. This procedure is called *shita-goshirae*, literally, "bottom-making." It consists of skinning the fish, removing the intestines, fins, and all the parts that are not used. The final cuts, of course, are left to the itamae.

The shikomi also learns to prepare all the other seafood, such as octopus, shrimp, etc., that itamae use to make sushi. And of course, the shikomi learns to cook rice and flavor it properly. This is probably the most important thing the shikomi learns, and he must learn it well.

The shikomi stage is crucial in the minarai's apprenticeship. Unless the minarai demonstrates to the head itamae that he can perform the shita-goshirae and rice making properly, he will never be raised to the next stage. Some minarai never advance beyond the shikomi stage and spend their entire working life as shikomi or seek employment elsewhere.

After the head itamae has ascertained your ability to perform the shikomi functions, you are promoted to *shimoita*. You stand behind the counter for the first time at this stage. For the first two or three months, the shimoita does not even make sushi for customers, unless a customer specifically asks that the newly-promoted shimoita make sushi for him.

Here we see the close relationship between the itamae and customers. It is the customers who make the itamae's work possible, and many take great pride in helping the minarai along the way.

At any rate, the shimoita just makes practice sushi for the first two or three months. After that, he does the work that any itamae does in making sushi, under the close supervision of the kami.

After about three years of this sort of journeyman itamae work, the shimoita is considered to be a full-fledged itamae. Only after this combined seven or eight years of apprenticeship can a minarai hire out to a sushi bar or restaurant as an itamae.

If a minarai changes shops during his apprenticeship, he goes to the stage below the stage he was employed at in the previous shop.

In Japan with its very close employer-employee relationship, an apprentice seldom changes position before his apprenticeship is over. This is gradually changing, however.

A very important part of an itamae's training is learning to get along with his customers. Although there is no formal training in this aspect of the work, the minarai is continually reminded that his livelihood depends on the good will of his customers and urged to at least learn several stories with which to entertain his customers. An itamae often considers himself as much an entertainer as culinary artist. Unfortunately, language is a big barrier in the United States for itamae trained in Japan.

Figure 7 illustrates what has been described above.

Recently, schools to train itamae in three months have opened in Japan. Traditionalists are very much against this. Making sushi is something learned with the entire body, and time is essential to getting a feel for it. Schools to train itamae can only be seen as an indication of the increasing demand for sushi.

FIGURE 7. STAGES IN THE ITAMAE APPRENTICESHIP

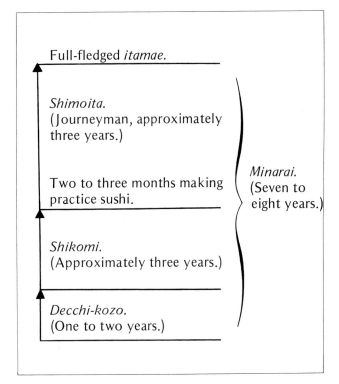

Full-fledged *itamae.*

Shimoita.
(Journeyman, approximately three years.)

Two to three months making practice sushi.

Shikomi.
(Approximately three years.)

Decchi-kozo.
(One to two years.)

Minarai.
(Seven to eight years.)

GRADING ITAMAE

As in many Japanese art forms, itamae are graded very closely. In the early 1960's, the itamae division of the Japanese culinary union set standards for those in the sushi-making business. The primary reason for the standards was to set salary guidelines, but since salary is closely tied to ability, it may be of interest to know something about grading itamae in Japan.

There are five major stages, from E (the lowest) to A (the highest); each stage has five levels.

The decchi-kozo stages are from E1 through E5. The level of decchi-kozo is determined only by the time worked. A person just starting his apprenticeship is placed in level E1, while an apprentice who has been employed close to two years is placed at level E5.

The shikomi stage is from D1 through D5. Some apprentices never get beyond this level.

From here on, the grading becomes rather blurred because of the subjectivity in evaluating the ability of the apprentice. The shimoita usually starts at the C1 level and progresses to either C3 or C4 before he is judged a full-fledged itamae. From that point on, everything depends on the itamae's ability.

Since there is a regular "course" the itamae goes through, it is possible to group itamae in terms of age. For example, all things being equal, itamae who start their apprenticeship immediately after high school and are about 28 years of age are usually in the B1 through B3 level. Those about 32 years of age are in the B3 through B5 level. Those over 36 years of age are in the A1 level or above. Master itamae are usually in the A2 or A3 levels.

To reach the A4 and A5 levels, a written test of not only sushi-making but of cooking in general, must be passed. These levels are sought primarily by those who write sushi books and lecture on the subject.

Figure 8 summarizes the above.

Keep in mind, however, that the standards for sushi in the United States are not as high as in Japan, and that there presently is no American itamae union.

FIGURE 8. ITAMAE GRADES

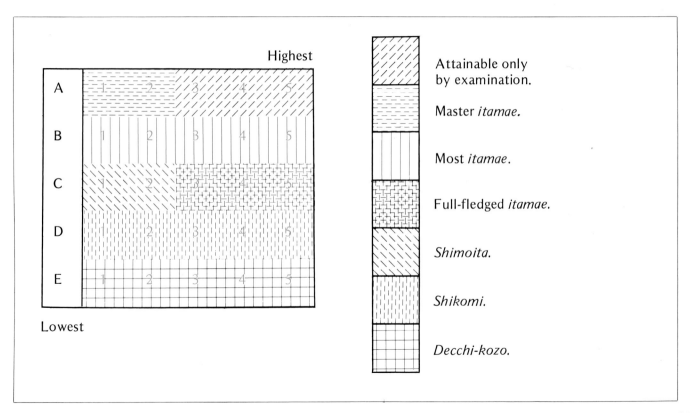

EVALUATING ITAMAE

An itamae should have spent at least seven years as an apprentice. This means he should have developed a certain attitude when he stands behind the sushi bar.

A good itamae does not stand too close to the counter. He will allow a certain amount of space between him and the counter. Standing too close to the counter is a sure sign of an itamae who is not a master of his art.

The itamae should keep his counter clean. He should keep the neta in the case so it always presents a pleasing appearance.

The primary skill of the itamae is the ability to use a knife. Each cut he makes should be a single downward stroke. There should be no "sawing" back and forth with the knife when the cut is made.

The itamae learns to cut by practicing on broad leaves called *haran*. The result of this cutting practice is *sasa*, the decorations used to set off sushi.

Sasa is presently made of plastic and is not cut individually by the itamae. But whether plastic sasa is used or not, the itamae should be able to cut a sasa for you to demonstrate his skill with a knife.

The standard sasa that an itamae might cut for you are shown in Figure 9. The first type (Figure 9A) is called *ken-zasa* ("sword" sasa) and the second major type of sasa (Figure 9B) is called *sekisho-zasa* ("barrier" sasa).

In addition to the two major types of sasa, some itamae have spent literally hundreds of hours cutting haran to demonstrate their ability with a knife. Figure 10 illustrates two sasa that were cut from a haran. You cannot, of course, expect an itamae to cut the sort of sasa shown in Figure 10, but it is not at all unreasonable to ask for and get a sasa such as shown in Figure 9 cut for you while you are sitting at the counter between bites of sushi.

(Illustrations of Figure 10 taken from *Sasa-giri Haran-giri Kyohon.*)

FIGURE 9. **THE TWO MAJOR TYPES OF SASA**

FIGURE 10. **EXAMPLES OF ELABORATE SASA**

9A. *Ken-zasa* ("Sword" Sasa)

9B. *Sekisho-zasa* ("Barrier" Sasa)

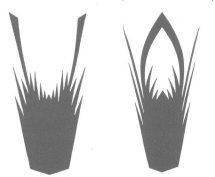

EATING SUSHI

EATING SUSHI

The most important thing about eating at a sushi bar is establishing a good relationship with the itamae. Rather than hopping from sushi bar to sushi bar, you should stick with one bar until you have some feel for how the itamae works. You will then have some standard of comparison when you go to another sushi bar.

Traditionally, and in the best sushi bars even today, the itamae did not write down the number and type of sushi that his customers ordered. It was considered part of the itamae's job to keep a running account in his head. This sometimes lead to mistakes in the bill, of course, but that is part of the art of the itamae. Just as the finest Oriental paintings and ceramics often have a slight flaw that enhances its value, so a mistake in the bill is part of the experience of eating at a sushi bar.

It is difficult, however, for Americans to take such a cavalier attitude towards what they consider a padded bill. Americans cannot understand why a sushi bill cannot be calculated with exactness. And it is, after all, their money. But this is where your relationship with the itamae comes in. If you cannot trust your itamae to keep an accurate account of your bill, can you trust him with what you put inside your stomach?

This is not to say that there are no itamae who are less than completely honest. But again, that is why your relationship with your itamae is so important. And as often as not, the mistake that the itamae makes will be in your favor, so in the long run things will be even.

So, you are now seated at the sushi bar. The itamae wipes the counter in front of you and places an *o-shibori* (wet towel), a cup of tea, and a handful of *shoga* (pickled ginger) on the wiped-off area. In some places the itamae will place a *geta*, a small tray with legs, on the counter in front of you. This is your personal "table" on which to place sushi.

The o-shibori may be hot or cold, depending on the season. Wipe your hands and face with the o-shibori. Be especially careful to wipe your hands; eating sushi is often done with the fingers. Let the warmth or the coolness of the o-shibori soak into your face and neck, and completely relax you. This is an important ritual in preparing to enjoy sushi. You are now ready to order. Some say you should start with *tamago-yaki* (egg omelet) to test the skill of the itamae because it is the only neta cooked by the itamae.

You will impress your itamae if you order in Japanese. Let us say you have ordered *maguro* (tuna). The itamae will place the finished pair of sushi on the counter in front of you with the maguro on top. Enjoy the bright red color of the maguro that contrasts so well with the white shari.

There is no "correct" way to eat sushi. Eat it any way that pleases you. You might place your right index finger over the front of the sushi and turn it over in one movement, as shown in Figure 11. If you do it this way, the sushi will be in the correct position without further movement. Or, you may wish to pick up the sushi, turn it over, place it back on the counter, and then pick it up in the correct position.

Whichever way you pick it up, the neta should be on the bottom. Grasp the sushi with your thumb and middle finger. Place your index finger lightly over the shari to hold it in place.

Dip the upper portion of the maguro in soy sauce. Do not let the soy sauce come in contact with the shari because the soy sauce will cause the shari to crumble.

Place the sushi on your tongue and begin chewing. The sushi is made to show off the neta but without the shari, the neta is not tasted to the fullest. The *wasabi* (horseradish) suddenly is apparent, adding further enjoyment to the sushi.

Eat the second sushi and savor its taste. When you are ready for another order of sushi, eat a little shoga. This cleanses your mouth of the taste of the sushi just eaten, and prepares you for your next order with a fresh mouth.

If you find the wasabi too strong, eat some shoga immediately, rather than trying to dilute the taste with tea. Then ask your itamae to put less wasabi on your next order.

You can also eat sushi with chopsticks, as illustrated in Figure 12.

You can also order *sashimi* (sliced raw fish) at the sushi bar. This will be placed in a small dish, artistically arranged. Use chopsticks to eat sashimi. Try alternating between orders of sushi and sashimi.

Most sushi bars offer *miso-shiru* (fermented soybean soup). This is tasty and very nutritious, and an excellent change of pace from both sushi and sashimi.

Probably the best advice that can be given about eating at a sushi bar is to respond, *"Omakase itashimasu,"* when asked what you wish to order. This phrase means, "I leave it up to you," or "What do you recommend?" Your itamae knows better than anyone which of his neta is freshest, and because he wants you to come back, will never give you bad advice.

If you want to get a little fancy, you might try asking for *o-agari* for tea, rather than the more usual *o-cha; o-hiya* for water, rather than the usual *o-mizu;* and *murasaki* for soy sauce, rather than *o-shoyu.* You should know, however, that in some places using the term murasaki, which literally means "purple," rather than o-shoyu, is considered an affectation.

When you are ready to pay your bill, ask for the *o-aiso.* The usual Japanese term for bill is *o-kanjo.* A little more formal term for bill is *dempyo.*

FIGURE 11. **EATING SUSHI BY HAND**

1. Place right index finger over the front of the sushi and tip over.

2. The sushi is on the way to being dipped in soy sauce.

3. Dip only the back (which is now in front) part of the *neta* into the soy sauce. Do not get soy sauce on the *shari* because then the *shari* will crumble.

4. Place the *neta* in your mouth so the neta lands on your tongue.

FIGURE 12. EATING SUSHI WITH CHOPSTICKS

1. Turn the sushi so the *neta* is on the side, rather than on top.

2. Grasp the sushi so that one chopstick touches the *neta* and the other touches the *shari*.

3. Dip the *neta* in the soy sauce.

4. Place the *neta* on your tongue.

SOME DON'TS

- Don't order other dishes (such as tempura) when you sit at the sushi bar. The odor from such dishes clash with the delicate odors of sushi. It is insulting to the itamae if you order something other than sushi or sashimi at the bar.

- Don't wear perfumes. The odor of the perfume will overpower the subtle aroma of the sushi.

- Don't dip the shari part of the sushi in the soy sauce.

- Don't put much (if any) wasabi in your soy sauce. Rely on your itamae to put the right amount of wasabi in your sushi.

Sushi is often called o-sushi. The "o" is an honorific added to nouns to indicate politeness. "O" is used with most common objects:

- *Hashi* (chopsticks) is o-hashi.
- *Chawan* (rice bowl) is o-chawan.

Any noun can be made more polite by adding the prefix "o." Show how civilized you are by adding the "o" to everything, even a word in English, such as tuna. Try asking for *o*-tuna (*o-maguro* in Japanese). Your itamae may look very surprised at this strange combination of terms, but he will understand.

EVALUATING SUSHI

Aside from omelet, shrimp, octopus, and a few other neta, all the materials from which sushi is made are used raw.

The neta should be brought fresh every day. This is why it is so important to find an itamae in whom you have confidence. You must be able to believe the itamae when he says all the neta is fresh. Of course, that also means you will probably have to pay a little more.

That is another reason why you should rely on the itamae for suggestions on what is in season and at its best.

Once you have ascertained that only the freshest materials are used, here are some secondary points you might take into consideration:

- Is the neta in the case lined up to present a pleasing appearance? Is everything clean and in the proper place, not only for the itamae to get to, but also so it can be seen by the customer? (The best sushi bars do not display neta in a case, but no bars in the United States presently follow this practice. The best sushi bars place their neta on a block of ice cut to fit the case. The next best bars place their neta on a bed of crushed ice. Most bars, however, place their neta in refrigerated cases.)
- Is the shari molded smoothly without finger grooves?
- Are the slices of raw fish *(sashimi)* on which the shari is placed, all of the same thickness? (There is no "standard" thickness; the head itamae (the *kami*) of each sushi bar sets the standard which the other itamae follow.)
- Is the *maki-zushi* sliced to the same thickness?

Traditionally, the perfect sushi was considered to be made with each grain of rice in the shari lined up in the same direction. No one, of course, has ever made sushi formed like that, and it really represents something forever elusive, like the "holy grail," sought by idealists.

An itamae's ability used to be evaluated by ordering omelet *(tamago yaki)*, because that is the only neta that is really "cooked." Unfortunately, shops that specialize in cooking nothing but omelets for sushi bars have opened in Japan, and they can no longer be used as a criteria to determine the abilities of the itamae in Japan. When the number of sushi bars in the United States increases, the business of cooking omelets for sushi bars can be expected to spread here too.

MISCELLANEOUS

DRINKS WITH SUSHI

The traditional drinks consumed with sushi are sake and tea. Over a period of centuries, these two types of drinks were found to best complement sushi. Today, however, beer seems to rival sake as the beverage to accompany sushi. Traditionalists do not agree; however, you should follow your own taste in this matter.

The following table lists the types of drinks and their suitability with sushi:

Drink	Suitability
Sake	Goes well with nigiri-zushi and sashimi (raw fish).
Tea	Goes well with all forms of sushi.
Beer	Not considered too suitable with sushi by traditionalists, but probably the most popular drink.
Distilled or mixed drinks	Not very suitable.

AMOUNT OF HORSERADISH (WASABI)

Traditionally, the Japanese have not cared for the taste of sharp or hot food, and this is reflected in the amount of horseradish used in sushi.

Japan was primarily a vegetarian country until the beginning of the Meiji period (1868-1912 A.D.). The meat they ate was mostly fish and wild game. For this reason, the Japanese sense of taste and smell was far more sensitive than that of people in countries where much meat is eaten.

The art of incense smelling developed in Japan to a high degree because of the Japanese sensitivity to odors. As recounted in works such as *Tales of Genji* by Lady Murasaki, professional "smell masters" used to mix incense for party guests to smell and guess the ingredients, and to judge the results.

An extra benefit of not eating much meat is the lack of body odor. Writing as late as 1905, Lafcadio Hearn remarked in surprise about how "sweet" a Japanese crowd smelled.

Japanese eating habits changed drastically after World War II, and a more Western diet is now followed. There is therefore an increasing desire among the Japanese for the taste of sharp food, and this is reflected in the amount of horseradish used in sushi.

The amount of horseradish used by the average person is still far less than the amount used by the average American, however.

A WORD ABOUT PRICES

It goes without saying that things are getting more expensive every day, and sushi can hardly be an exception. If you and a friend each have four or five pairs of sushi and several bottles of sake or beer, you should not be surprised to receive a bill in excess of fifty dollars.

Sushi bars in Japan are placed in one of three classes:

- Top class *(jo-ryu)*.
- Middle class *(chu-ryu)*.
- Third class *(san-ryu)*.

Only the top and middle class sushi bars are considered worth frequenting. Generally, prices in Japan (as of 1983) can be said to be in the following ranges:

Middle class—from $2.50 to $6.00/pair of sushi.

Top class—from $4.00 to $12.00/pair of sushi. Happily, prices in the United States tend to be somewhat lower than in Japan.

Some American hotels and restaurants that cater to Japanese tourists seem to have two prices for sushi. You needn't worry, however, because it is the Japanese who are charged the higher prices.

If you are concerned about cost, order a fixed combination of sushi called *moriawase-zushi* ("mix" and "combine"). It will be listed on the menu with the price and the types of sushi you will receive. When you order moriawase-zushi, you must sit at a table located away from the sushi bar. The bar is reserved for customers who order sushi individually. It is best not to order moriawase-zushi at a restaurant where there is no sushi bar even if it is on the menu; sushi is usually of secondary importance at such places.

NUTRITIONAL VALUE

One of the pleasures of eating sushi is knowing how good it is for us. All the materials used to make sushi are fresh so their nutritional value is not lost. Aside from *toro,* the fatty cut of tuna, almost none of the materials contain fat or oil. They are high in protein, low in calories, and filled with vitamins and minerals. The vinegar added to the rice has anti-bacterial qualities, and the Japanese believe it lowers high blood pressure. What more can you ask of a food?

FISH MOTIFS

The tea cups in most sushi bars have a fish motif. Many are decorated with text. The text that decorates the cup shown in Figure 13 uses the names of fish as homonyms. The characters that are the names of fish can be determined by the fish radical (魚) to the left of the characters:

鮪 is the way to write *maguro* (tuna).

鯖 is the way to write *saba* (mackerel).

etc.

The characters used above to illustrate how fish characters are written are the simplest way to write the characters. Sushi bars in Japan, however, where everyone can read Chinese characters, are decorated with the characters written in a more flowery and less easily identifiable way. The back cover of this book is printed with the names of fish set in a type font that is favored for use with sushi-related subjects.

The text that decorates the cup shown in Figure 13 can be read in several ways. It can be read as a humorous story about two fish, an *ayu* (smelt) and a *koi* (carp), or an equally humorous story about a girl named Ayu and a boy named Koi. The text contains at least one character that the writer invented and whose meaning must be surmised from the parts of the character that comprise it and the context within which it is used. One way in which the text can be read is:

FIGURE 13.   **TEA CUP USED IN SUSHI BARS**

Ayu and Koi kissed. Ayu became pregnant, causing Ayu's boyfriend to cry exceedingly. Koi's master chastised Koi, but nothing could be done. Ayu's ex-boyfriend began drinking to seek solace. Years passed and he became as black as (the ink from) an octopus. Eventually everyone died so all ended happily.

The above is only one of the ways in which the text can be read, although none makes really good sense because the text is a play on the names of fish. As an example, the fish *kisu* is of the same family as the cod and haddock, but its name is also the Japanese way of pronouncing the English word "kiss." For Japanese, the very vagueness of the text and the many meanings that can be read into it adds to the fun of trying to decipher what is written.

Sushi bars often have signs and other decorations that consist of the names of fish. Figure 14 is a photograph of a *noren* with such decoration. *Noren* are short "curtains" traditionally hung over

FIGURE 14. A SIGN CONSISTING OF THE NAMES OF FISH

FIGURE 15. A BLOCK-PRINT BY HIROSHIGE

the door to advertise shops. In feudal times they were given by the owner of a shop to faithful employees who were considered worthy of setting out on their own. The decoration on this *noren* cannot be read with meaning; it consists of the names of fish grouped together in no particular order.

Fish are celebrated in Japanese art. Figure 15 is one of a series of woodblock prints devoted solely to fish by the famed artist, Hiroshige. This print was created early in the 19th century.

THE ULTIMATE IN SUSHI EATING

The best sushi bars in Japan do not have a case in which the neta is displayed. You are assumed to be knowledgeable enough about the neta to ask for what you want, with the absolute assurance that it is the best obtainable. You should, of course, always rely on the judgement of the itamae regarding what is best for that day.

Sushi is very expensive at these top-class bars. If you have to ask how much it is, you cannot afford it. Go elsewhere. But *tsu* (sushi gourmets) wax eloquent over their experiences at such bars.

GLOSSARY

GLOSSARY

agari - special sushi term for tea; usually prefixed with *o*, *o-agari*.

aiso - special sushi term for bill; usually prefixed with *o*, *o-aiso*.

ama-kuchi - vinegared rice usually used to make *inari-zushi*.

anakyu-maki - "sea-eel and cucumber roll." Sea-eel and cucumber placed on vinegared rice and rolled in a sheet of dried seaweed.

cha - usual Japanese term for tea; usually prefixed with *o*, *o-cha*.

chirashi-zushi - "scattered sushi." Vinegared rice placed in a box, on top of which is placed fish or other ingredients. Eaten from the box using chopsticks.

choko-sake - small cup to hold sake; usually prefixed with *o*, *o-choko-sake*.

chu-maki - "middle roll." *Maki-zushi* made with a moderate amount of vinegared rice on which is placed two or three different types of ingredients.

debabocho - type of knife used by the sushi-maker; 6 - 8 inches long. It looks like:

decchi-kozo - beginning apprentice sushi-maker.

dempyo - formal Japanese term for bill; usually prefixed with *o*, *o-dempyo*.

dosa - the body posture of the sushi-maker while standing and working behind the counter. Refers to both the spiritual and physical bearing of the sushi-maker which sushi experts use to judge the excellence of the sushi-maker.

edomae-zushi - "in-front-of-Edo (Bay) sushi." Same as *nigiri-zushi*.

futo-maki - "thick roll." *Maki-zushi* made with much vinegared rice and up to five different types of ingredients.

gari - special sushi term for pickled ginger.

geta - small stand on which your sushi order is placed.

hana-zushi - residue from making *tofu (tofu-no-*

okara) placed on vinegared rice.

handai - tray (often round) on which to place an order of "mixed" sushi. Prefixed with a term that indicates how large the tray is: *ichinin-mai* = order for one person; *sannin-mai* = order for three persons; *gonin-mai* = order for five persons; etc.

haran - a type of broad leaf used to practice cutting, and from which the decorative designs *(sasa)* served with sushi used to be made.

hashi - chopsticks; usually prefixed with *o, o-hashi.*

hashi-oki - "chopstick stand." Small, usually porcelain, implement on which chopsticks not being used are placed; usually prefixed with *o, o-hashi-oki.*

hitsu - large container to hold the vinegared rice that the sushi-maker uses to make sushi. Traditionally made of wood, but increasingly made of plastic. Usually prefixed with *o, o-hitsu.*

hiya - special sushi term for water; usually prefixed with *o, o-hiya.*

hocho - general term for the knife used by the sushi-maker. There are three types of *hocho: yanagi, takokiri,* and *debabocho.*

hoso-maki - "thin roll." *Maki-zushi* made with only one ingredient in the middle.

itamae - sushi-maker.

inari-zushi - deep-fried bean-curd *(abura-age)* stuffed with vinegared rice.

kami - the head or lead sushi-maker.

kanjo - usual Japanese term for bill; usually prefixed with *o, o-kanjo.*

kappa-maki - "*kappa* roll." Sliced cucumbers placed on vinegared rice and rolled in a sheet of dried seaweed. A *kappa* is a half-frog, half-human creature said to live in water.

karifonia maki - "California roll." Sushi developed in California, almost always containing avocado.

kikai-maki - "mechanical roll." Special sushi term referring to *maki-zushi* in general.

kokuchi-aji - vinegared rice usually used to make *chirashi-zushi.*

kozara - "small dish." Dish to hold the soy sauce in which to dip sushi.

kyuri-maki - "cucumber roll." Same as *kappa-maki.*

maguro-maki - "tuna roll." Same as *tekka-maki.*

makisu - a device made of bamboo strips loosely tied together and used to make *maki-zushi.*

maki-zushi - "rolled sushi." General term for ingredients placed on vinegared rice and rolled in a sheet of dried seaweed.

manaita - counter the sushi-maker works on.

minarai - general term for apprentice. The stages a *minarai* goes through before becoming a full-fledged sushi-maker are: *decchi-kozo, shikomi,* and *shimoita.*

miso-shiru - nutritious broth made of soy-bean paste.

mizu - usual Japanese term for water; usually prefixed with *o, o-mizu.*

moriawase-zushi - "mixed sushi." A combination of various types of sushi.

mura-choko - special sushi term for *kozara,* the dish to hold the soy sauce in which to dip sushi.

murasaki - special sushi term for soy sauce.

mushi-zushi - "steamed sushi." Vinegared rice with fish or other ingredients on top, placed in a box with a screen or holes in the bottom. The box is placed over boiling water to steam the contents.

nakaita - sushi-makers other than the head sushi-maker in bars where there are more than three sushi-makers.

nama-nare-zushi - a development of *nare-zushi* still made today. The fish is used raw with the rice made "acidy" with vinegar.

nare-zushi - "ripened sushi." Forerunner of modern sushi. Rice was used to ferment the fish, after which the rice was discarded.

neta - ingredients on which the vinegared rice is placed to make sushi.

nigiri-zushi - "grasped sushi." Hand-molded pieces of vinegared rice placed on fish or other ingredient.

noren - short decorated "curtains" traditionally hung

over the door of a shop as an advertisement.

nori-maki - "seaweed roll." General term for ingredients placed on vinegared rice and rolled in a sheet of dried seaweed. Same as *maki-zushi*.

o - an honorific prefix added to nouns.

okashi-zushi - "confectionary sushi." Small pieces of molded vinegared rice with fish or other ingredients on top, arranged to form a design.

"omakase-itashi-masu" - a good reply to a request for your order; means, "I leave it up to you," or "What do you recommend?".

oshi-zushi - "pressed sushi." Vinegared rice placed in a box, on top of which fish or other ingredients are placed. The rice/fish is pressed in the box, removed, and cut into bite-size pieces, like a cake.

saibashi - chopstick-like tool used by the sushi-maker to dig things out or to place things on sushi.

-san - an honorific suffix added to names.

sasa - green ornamental designs to set off sushi. Used to be cut from *haran* leaves, but now are usually made of plastic.

sashimi - sliced raw fish.

shari - rice flavored with vinegar, sake, salt, and sugar.

shibori - "wring-out." The damp cloth with which to wipe your hands and face before eating sushi. Can be warm or cold, depending on the season. Usually prefixed with *o*, *o-shibori*.

shibori-ire - small bamboo holder in which the *o-shibori* is placed; usually prefixed with *o*, *o-shibori-ire*.

shikomi - second rung of the sushi apprenticeship.

shimoita - journeyman sushi-maker.

shitagoshirae - "bottom-making." Consists of skinning a fish and removing all the intestines, fins, and other parts that will not be used.

shoyu - usual Japanese term for soy sauce; usually prefixed with *o*, *o-shoyu*.

sudare-maki - 1) same as *makisu*. 2) same as *maki-zushi*, *nori-maki*, and *kikai-maki*.

su-maki - "vinegar roll." Vinegared rice rolled in a sheet of dried seaweed without ingredients.

takohiki-hocho - type of knife used by sushi-maker; about a foot long. It looks like:

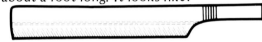

tane - same as neta.

tekka-maki - "*tekka* roll." Raw tuna placed in vinegared rice and rolled in a sheet of dried seaweed. *Tekka-ba* means "gambling den." This sushi probably received its name because gamblers wanted food they could eat without disturbing their game.

temaki-zushi - ingredients placed in vinegared rice, hand rolled in a sheet of dried seaweed, and served unsliced.

teppo-maki - "rifle roll." Dried gourd shavings placed on vinegared rice and rolled in a sheet of dried seaweed.

tori-zara - medium-size dish in which to place sushi. Often used to serve children who cannot reach the counter.

tsu - sushi expert.

tsuke-dai - counter.

usu-aji - vinegared rice usually used to make *nigiri-zushi*.

wasabi - horseradish.

yanagi-hocho - type of knife used by the sushi-maker; about a foot long. It looks like:

SQUID *Ika*

Squid is usually served raw but it has also been prepared by boiling in soy sauce and sugar, and also marinated in a sugar and vinegar solution.

SALMON *Shake*

Salmon is usually served slightly smoked and is popular among Americans who are used to lox. This is a good sushi with which to become initiated into the world of sushi.

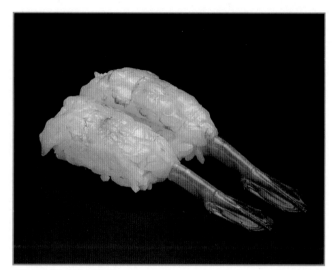

SWEET SHRIMP *Ama-ebi*

Sweet shrimp is usually served raw and the fresher it is, the better. It is meaty and firm, and has a sweetness you would not ordinarily associate with shrimp, especially in a raw state. The head of the sweet shrimp, cooked in oil, is also served.

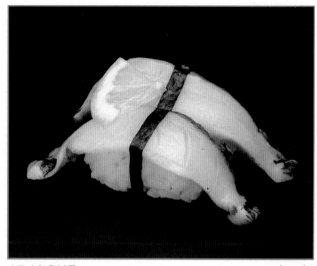

ABALONE *Awabi*

Abalone used to be steamed in salt water, but is now usually served raw. Cut into thin slices, it is crunchy and very satisfying.

CALIFORNIA ROLL *Kashu-maki*

California roll is proof that the world of sushi is constantly growing. *Kashu* is the Japanese term for California, and *maki* means "roll." Made with avocados, crab meat, cucumbers, and other ingredients, California roll is popular among Americans and very exotic for Japanese.

FISH EGGS ON KELP *Kazuno-ko Kombu*

Fish eggs on kelp are preserved in salt water and then kept in lightly salted water until served. Shavings of dried bonito *(katsuobushi)* are frequently tied to the fish eggs on kelp with a strip of dried seaweed *(nori)* to bring out the taste.

TUNA *Maguro*

A sushi bar would be out of business if it was out of tuna. *Maguro* is cut from the leanest part of the tuna, the part closest to the spine. Cuts closer to the belly of the tuna have other names.

KING CRAB *Kani*

The legs of the King Crab are used to make this sushi. It is sweet and firm, and a good contrast to the vinegared rice on which it is placed.

SHRIMP *Ebi*

HERRING (GIZZARD SHAD) *Kohada*

Shrimp is one of the most popular sushi. It is one of the few in which the form of the living creature is retained. The beautiful color of the shrimp is brought out when it is cooked. The shell of the tail is left to enhance the "shrimp-ness."

The taste of the herring is hidden so the sushi-maker must work to bring it out. This is why *tsu* (sushi experts) use herring as one of the criteria for evaluating the skill of a sushi-maker.

MACKEREL *Saba*

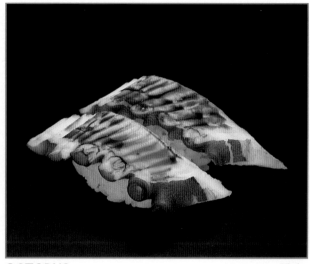

OCTOPUS *Tako*

Mackerel is usually served vinegared, but is also served raw. It is prepared with part of the inner skin left intact. Mackerel is abundant in the waters off the Japanese archipelago, and is a traditional Japanese favorite.

Octopus is usually served boiled. It is a meaty complement to the vinegared rice. Lemon juice is often used in place of soy sauce to bring out the taste.

JUMBO CLAM *Miru-gai*

The tasty part of the jumbo clam is the long muscular siphon that extends beyond the ocean floor when the shell is buried in the sand. This part of the clam is lean, crisp, and quite tasty.

EGG OMELET *Tamago-yaki*

Egg omelet is often used to evaluate the skill of the sushi-maker. This no longer has meaning in Japan because most sushi shops there purchase their egg omelet from shops that specialize in cooking it.

HALIBUT (FLOUNDER) *Hirame*

The best parts of the halibut are the narrow strips along the upper and lower sides next to the fin. A few drops of lemon juice greatly enhance this sushi. It is the most popular of the "white meat" *(shiromi).*

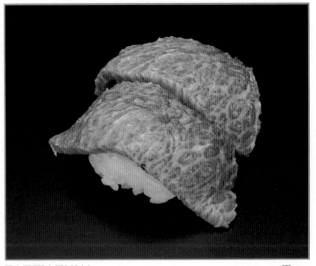

FATTY TUNA *Toro*

Fatty tuna is the meat of the tuna cut closer to the belly of the fish, which contains more fat than the flesh closer to the spine. Try both tuna *(maguro)* and fatty tuna for contrast.

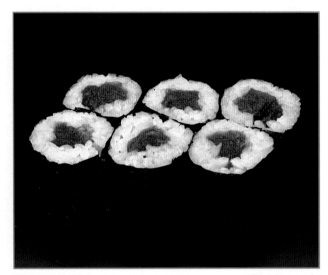

TUNA ROLL *Tekka-maki*

Tekka-ba means gambling den in Japanese. This sushi gets its name from the fact that Japanese gamblers wanted a food they could eat without being distracted from their game. In its present form, this sushi consists of a piece of tuna and vinegared rice rolled in dried seaweed *(nori)*.

SALMON ROE *Ikura*

The Japanese term for salmon roe, *ikura*, is said to be derived from the Russian *ikura*, meaning fish roe or caviar. The dried seaweed *(nori)* used to make this sushi complements the taste of the salmon roe.

CUCUMBER ROLL *Kappa-maki*

SEA EEL *Anago*

A *kappa* is a mythical half-human, half-frog-like creature that lives in water. It is not clear how such a creature came to be associated with cucumbers, but perhaps the reason is that both are green. Cucumber roll is a refreshing sushi that is an excellent change-of-pace after sushi made of richer ingredients.

Sea eel is a test of the sushi-maker's skill. It is cooked in a mixture of water, *sake*, soy sauce, and sugar, and then brushed with a thick sweet sauce. Horseradish *(wasabi)* is not used with sea eel.

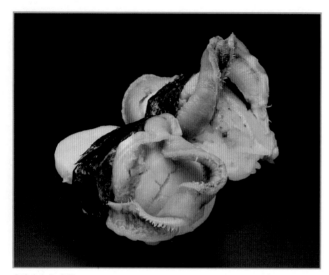

SCALLOP *Hotate-gai*

YELLOWTAIL *Hamachi*

Scallop is cooked in a mixture of water, *sake*, soy sauce, and sugar. Horseradish *(wasabi)* is not used with scallop, which has a taste unlike any other sushi.

Hamachi is the name given to cultivated yellowtail. When caught in the ocean, it is called *buri*. Some species of yellowtail are oily and similar in taste to fatty tuna *(toro)*.

SEA URCHIN *Uni*

FISH EGGS *Kazuno-ko*

Sea urchin is placed on top of vinegared rice and held in place with dried seaweed *(nori)* which extends beyond the rice. Sea urchin is an acquired taste, and while some refuse to even try it, others think it is the tastiest of sushi.

The fish eggs are solidified with a substance called *shohakuzai* and then kept in salt water until served. Shavings of dried bonito *(katsuobushi)* are frequently tied to the fish eggs with a strip of dried seaweed *(nori)* to bring out the taste of the fish eggs.

FLYING-FISH ROE *Tobigo*

Flying-fish roe is similar to the roe of crab, but slightly less sweet, and also a little smaller. Because crab roe is so expensive, some unscrupulous sushi bars serve flying-fish roe as crab roe.

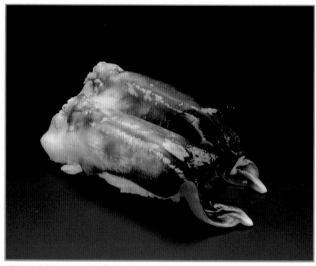

BLACK CLAM (COCKLE) *Tori-gai*

Tori in Japanese means "chicken" and *gai* means "shellfish." The Japanese associate black clams with chickens because of the resemblance to a chicken's beak.

RED CLAM *Akagai*

Red clam is not crunchy and yet not soft. It has a refreshing taste that is excellent as a change of pace from sushi with a heavier taste. Many people like a drop or two of lemon on this sushi.

HALFBEAK *Sayori*

This is an ocean fish that is closely allied to the flying fish. If you are served this sushi, you can contemplate that while it was alive, it used to leave the ocean for a few moments and soar through the air before returning to the water. Good with beer or *sake*.

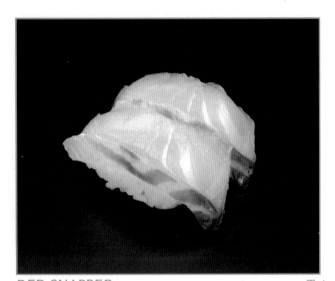

RED SNAPPER   *Tai*

In addition to being a popular neta, the red snapper is very good as *sashimi*, eaten raw by itself. In Japanese, the word for felicitations is "mede-*tai*," so *tai* is also frequently cooked whole with bamboo skewers to hold its shape, and served on festive occasions.

RADISH LEAVES   *Kaiwari*

Dried bonito shavings are often included with radish leaves to create this sushi. It is refreshing in taste and an excellent change of pace after a heavy sushi such as *toro*, or after a drink.

MANTIS PRAWN *Shako*

The mantis prawn is usually served boiled. It has a taste somewhere between the eel and shrimp.

PICKLED GIANT RADISH *Oshinko*

Oshinko is giant radish pickled in fermented soybean paste which gives the radish its yellow color. A few pieces of *oba* (beefsteak leaves) are usually included with the *oshinko* to make this sushi.

ABOUT THE AUTHOR

Kenji Kumagai was born in Aomori, Japan. When he was 15 years of age, he was apprenticed to sushi master Shiraishi who ran a sushi bar named Sushi-Yoshi in Tokyo. After two years, Mr. Kumagai transferred to a shop named Kiyo-zushi, where he completed his apprenticeship under master Ito.

Starting at the bottom of the apprenticeship ladder as a *decchi-kozo,* Mr. Kumagai was promoted to *shikomi,* then *shimoita,* and was recognized as a full-fledged *itamae* (sushi-maker) in 1962.

Mr. Kumagai was employed at various sushi bars in the Tokyo area until 1976, when he was recruited by the owner of the Eigiku Restaurant in Los Angeles, and made head *itamae* at the sushi bar there. After a year, he became head *itamae* at the sushi bar in the Thousand Cranes Restaurant located within the New Otani Hotel.

Because of Mr. Kumagai's over 25 years of experience in the world of sushi, he is regarded as a *sempai* (senior) by the *itamae* in the Southern California area.